For those who want to become Richer beyond their Imaginations

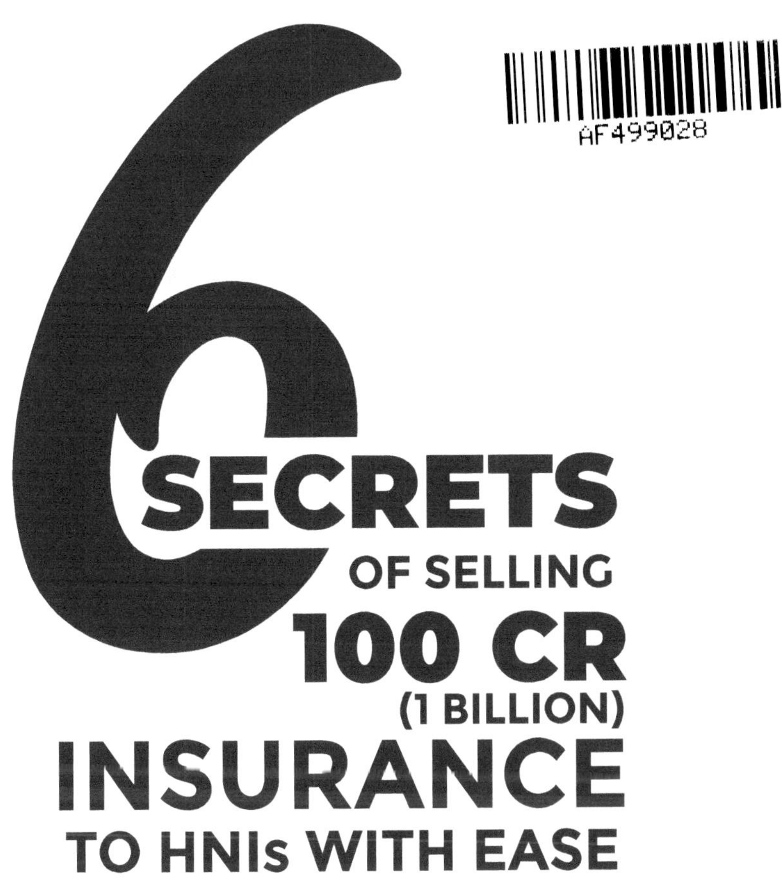

6 SECRETS OF SELLING 100 CR (1 BILLION) INSURANCE TO HNIs WITH EASE

For those who want to become Richer beyond their Imaginations

6 SECRETS OF SELLING 100 CR (1 BILLION) INSURANCE TO HNIs WITH EASE

RANDHIR BHALLA

Published Internationally by
Pendown Press
Powered by Gullybaba.com

PENDOWN PRESS

Powered by **Gullybaba Publishing House Pvt. Ltd.,**
An ISO 9001 & ISO 14001 Certified Co.,
Regd. Office: 2525/193, 1st Floor, Onkar Nagar-A, Tri Nagar, Delhi-110035
Ph.: 09350849407, 09312235086
E-mail: info@pendownpress.com
Branch Office: 1A/2A, 20, Hari Sadan, Ansari Road, Daryaganj, New Delhi-110002
Ph.: 011-45794768
Website: PendownPress.com

First Edition: 2021

ISBN: 978-93-90557-15-8

Layout Design: Pendown Press Publishing

Dedication

Dedicated to my late father
Shri. K.C. Bhalla who was a proud LICian.

He imparted lots of value in my life and ingrained in my thought process a sense of commitment and gratification as he always used to recite Kabir's Couplet (Doha)...

''साई इतना दीजिये, जा मे कुटुम समाय।
मैं भी भूखा न रहूँ, साधु न भूखा जाय।।''

"God give me only that much in which my
family can survive
I do not remain hungry and the guest should
also not go hungry."

Contents

About The Book

Let me tell you one secret! Every insurance seller dreams of selling at least One Big Insurance worth Rs.100.00 cr (1 Billion) during lifetime as this can set him apart from the crowd and place him into an entirely different league.

But only a few can achieve this lifetime dream.

In this book, Author Randhir Bhalla narrates his years of experience dealing with HNIs, decodes their deep-rooted secret desires and then finally, work out methods to present them offers that are truly **"Irresistible, Difficult to ignore or to put them aside."**

The Book reveals **Six Golden Secrets** of selling high value insurance to HNIs with ease as taught in **Top Busincss Schools of the World.**

The book lays down a process to help you emerge from the clutches of being an ordinary insurance seller to an extraordinary one.

This is the powerful guide to help insurance sellers achieve their lifetime aspiration and become richer beyond their imaginations.

If you are reading this, you could be one of the chosen ones!

Central Theme of this Book is
"It's all about Value creation !!!"

''धन्धा वैल्यू का खेल है मेरे दोस्त!!!''

About The Author

Randhir Bhalla & Associates are Senior Engineers, Chartered and Cost Accountants.

Randhir Bhalla is an author and speaker at forums that include FICCI, ASSOCHAM (New Delhi) and FKCCI (Federation Karnataka Chamber Of Commerce & Industries, Bengaluru).

He is regarded as India's Top Financial Business Continuity Planner.

The customized Financial Business Continuity Plans designed by him add lots of value to the Business Enterprises, their Promoters, Collaborators, Investors and key persons in the organizations

He firmly believes that P > R i.e. Protection is always Bigger than Returns.

In his unique style, he structures Big Insurance Plans for HNIs to transfer their Risks to Insurance Cos. and help them live stress-free lives.

You can connect with the Author on

Email id- randhirbhalla1950@gmail.com

Mb: 9376117563, 8141117563

Preface

My father Mr. K.C. Bhalla who worked with LIC of India throughout his life, taught me:

"Selling Insurance is a difficult job
and that one who can sell life insurance
can sell anything."

And here I am. Trying to follow his footsteps and teach you how you can sell insurance worth Rs. 100.00 cr (1 Billion) and more to HNIs with ease.

Yes. It is possible. If I can do it, surely you too can.

I want you, my readers, to understand that the content I am sharing in this book is based on my 45 years of hardcore experience working with HNIs.

It is the crux of everything. I have learned, unlearned, perfected and implemented over the years.

Using this knowledge I have achieved unbelievable success in my life.

This Book is written for all my Friends, Colleagues, Development Officers and other Senior Officials of the Insurance industry across the world whom I know or otherwise.

I sincerely hope this Book will add great value in your personal and professional lives and make you richer than what you ever imagined failing which the very purpose of writing it will remain unfulfilled.

My desire is to make all readers of this book truly **"World Class Champions."**

Read this Book with lots of belief, passion and enthusiasm.

May God bless you all.

Chapter 1

What a Life!

My Journey

Unlike many others, my journey is not from **Rags to Riches.**

Born in a reasonably well-placed family, I was given adequate education and value in my life. During the last 45 years, I had opportunities to work at the highest level of the organizations (CEOs) and have interacted with (ultra) rich HNIs.

By grace of God my career graph has always been from being **Rich to Richer.**

My Current Lifestyle

- Working at my own pace.
- Sufficient time for me, my family and friends.
- The priority of my life ranking from 1 to 10 is my "Health".

- Living a life of lifelong financial independence and dignity.
- Enjoy four vacations in a year.

I travel across the world and interact with Top Insurance Sellers.

Do you want to know how I manage to live this kind of lifestyle?

It's all because I have learnt the Art and Science of creating value in the lives of my HNI customers.

Chapter 2

I Am Here By Choice

Friends, unlike most insurance sellers, I am in this industry by choice and not by chance.

I use life insurance products as tools to Mitigate Corporate Risks. This is essentially a process of Identifying, Valuing and Transferring the Business Risks to the insurance providers.

These are perfect tools that can add value to the Corporate world.

All these help me sell **Big Life Insurance.**

Chapter 3

A 30-Second Introduction That Sets Me Apart From The Crowd

This 30 seconds Introduction/Tagline–Describing USP sets me apart from the crowd.

My clients perceive me as an **Expert** and not as a **Commodity.**

"Hi,

My name is Randhir.

Randhir Bhalla.

My job is to help people to take informed decisions in their lives.

I tell people what most others don't.

I don't tell people how to become Super Rich.

Instead, I inform them as to how they should protect their hard-earned money.

Our Clients do not hire us to make them Rich.

They hire us to ensure that they will never be Poor…

We are India's Top Financial Business Continuity Planner.

We manage your Risks."

Chapter 4

What Our Clients And Associates Say About Us

"I have personally witnessed how a Proposal of Rs. 210 cr was closed by Mr. Randhir Bhalla effortlessly. His techniques are absolutely unique and priceless. Listening to him is just a terrific experience."

-Ravindra Kumar,

Regional Manager, LIC of India

Dear Randhir ji,

It was a pleasure meeting you.

You have a good business plan which can meet an important requirement that most family-owned enterprises tend to overlook.

Wishing you great success...

–Rajesh,

Managing Director, Lockheed Martin (A Fortune 500 Co.–Largest Fighter Aircraft Manufacturer of the world)

I am a proud member of Rs. 100.00 cr (1 Billion) Club.

Just amazing feelings.

The Business Continuity Plan customized by Mr. Randhir Bhalla is at its Best when your Business is at its Worst.

Too good to believe!!!

–P. S. Rajiv,

Business Owner

The unique skills displayed by Mr. Randhir Bhalla are absolute thought provoking.

We have done it. No hesitation to recommend strongly.

– Krupesh Thakkar,

MD, M/S Rushil Decor Ltd.

Big Sales during lockdown period is something amazing.

Mr. Randhir Bhalla has truly mastered an ART of selling big ticket insurance even to unknowns.

His product presentation brings about huge value for the customers.

Just Brilliant!!!!

–Amit Kumar,

Br. M. LIC

Chapter 5

A Real Life Case Study

Before we go further, I want to share a Case Study which is important for you to know so that you can understand the technical part of this content.

Friends, during the last 15 years I have sold quite a few big insurances to HNIs. The highest ever was a sum assured of Rs. 210.00 cr with a regular premium of Rs.163.00 Lakhs.

A Real Life Case Study

I was introduced by one of my well-wishers to an owner of a successfully-run business enterprise.

A Brief Background

- This is a mid-size manufacturing unit having Sales Revenue and the Net Profits around Rs.500.00 Cr and Rs.50.00 Cr respectively.

- The company has no loan liabilities. Instead, carries a huge cash surplus deployed in Bank FDs or in other short term financial investment instruments.
- Business is growing at the rate of more than 20% year-on-year (YOY).
- This is 17 years old family-owned company managed by father and son aged 65 and 40 respectively.
- Son (Managing Director) is very well qualified from the Top Business School of the World and is practically running the entire show.
- He is a person with big ambitions and not afraid to take risks for the sake of exponential growth.
- His passion makes him to travel across the world to look for opportunities.
- As a part of Risk Mitigation Strategy, he has secured himself with an Insurance cover of Rs.35.00 cr.

My introduction was given as a Corporate Risk Manager, someone who can help them protect their Business Risks.

They liked the Tagline on my Business Card viz.

"Our Clients do not hire us to make them rich. They hire us to make sure that they will never be 'Poor'."

They eventually decided to give me an audience with the mixed feelings as to how I can help them further.

What Happened In That Meeting?

After exchanging initial pleasantries, there came the first objection.

Asked the young Promoter,

"Mr. Randhir Bhalla please tell us as to how you can help a successfully managed business like ours carrying presumably No Risks Whatsoever?

We have no loan liabilities and have a large amount of surplus resources at our command to fall back upon in case of eventuality.

Furthermore, we have put in place full proof systems with adequate checks and balances.

Our human resources are unmatchable and can meet with any unforeseen challenges.

Besides, I have covered my personal risks with the help of life insurance worth Rs.35.00 cr."

This was truly a bomb shell to drag any insurance seller into a corner as one would find it difficult to propose a solution that can turn out to be an Irresistible Offer.

Reading this I am sure like many other readers you must also be puzzled as much as I was at that point of time.

The Million $ question in front of me was

How can one contribute value in the lives of such successful people who are not falling short of anything in their lives?

Eager to know what I did next?

I closed the deal and collected an Annual Premium of Rs.121 Lakhs!!

How??

I knew this question would certainly come, and that's why I'm here to share my knowledge with you.

Before I disclose as to how did I accomplish a truly challenging assignment let me share a little gyan (ज्ञान) with you that will set a framework to sail through such daunting challenges.

Keep reading... (You have to dive deeper)

Chapter 6

Marketing v/s Selling

Don't forget these Golden Rules. Set your Understandings Right.

Simply put, Marketing is not Selling. It is a presentation of your product/services in a way that would create an environment where your buyer would like to buy your product or services from you.

Marketing does not create sales. It simply creates awareness about your product/services and promises to add value. It is only what you do after marketing that brings sales.

If you want to sell in bulk you need to influence the buyer's mind and, therefore, you need to understand his mindset.

Remember, Selling is all about Telling, Helping and Informing with Relaxation.

It should give new meaning to your sales process by way of listening, helping with a commitment to add value supported by positive body language.

The more you tell, the more you sell.

Remember, HNIs never like to be sold. They like to buy.

Never try **Desperate Selling** by being **Pushy or Salesy** with them. Instead, create an Environment where they would like to **"Buy".**

Help them to take decisions by presenting solutions which are truly **Unique.**

It should be truly a **Driven Selling** with a passion to solve the problems.

Create pain by magnifying their problems and act like a doctor.

Never manipulate.

Only influence.

Chapter 7

2 Ways of Marketing

1. Hand Grenade Marketing

Hand Grenade Marketing is what we have been doing right NOW to sell insurance i.e. making offers to anybody and everybody without understanding the Buyer's Deep-Rooted Secret Desires (Needs).

2. Sniper Marketing

Sniper Marketing is one where your potential buyers are targeted, well defined (Your ideal customers are those who can match your value system) and clear strategies are worked out to add ultimate value in their lives for their eventual transformation into satisfied buyers.

Chapter 8

Desperate v/s Driven Selling

What is desperate selling?

Desperate Selling is one when the objective is to chase the numbers disregarding the value being offered.

Driven selling is all about passion to add tons of value in the buyer's life.

It's never a Desperate Selling. If you want to sell more or in bulk, you have to stop selling. Create a buying environment.

Federico Fellini, an Italian Film Director and Screenwriter once said, "There is no end. There is no beginning. There is only the passion of life."

Learn to sell with passion.

Chapter 9

Current Scenario

- ALREADY WEAK ECONOMY becoming weaker; instead of slower growth, the economy is expected to contract in the next two quarters.

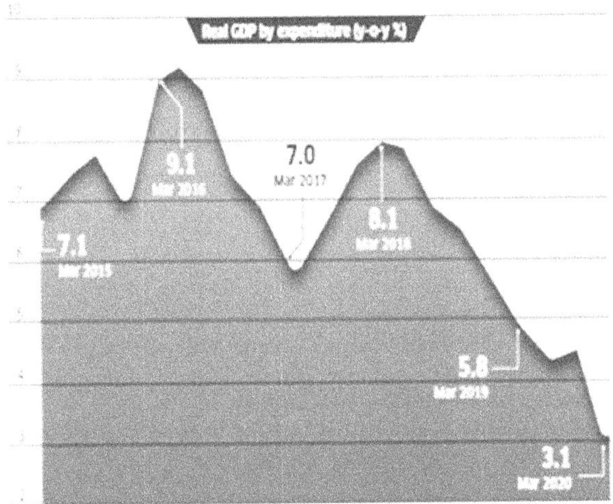

- How to survive the coming recession

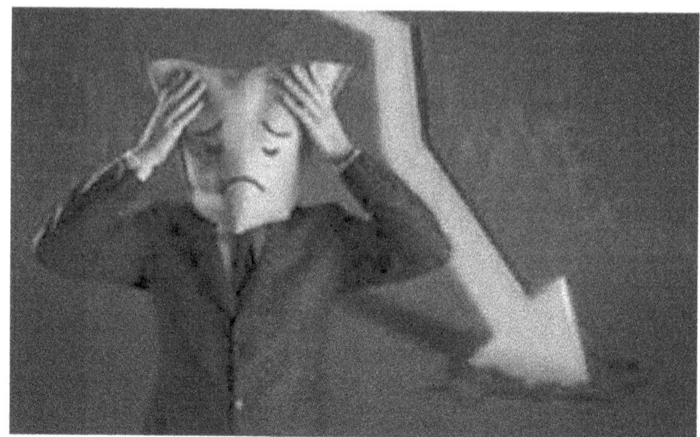

- India is among worst performing economies in the world; stimulus inadequate: Abhijit Banerjee

Source: The Economic Times, 30th Sep 2020

- 82% Indians bear financial brunt of corona virus pandemic survey.

Source: The Economic Times, 7th June 2020

- Global economy to plunge into worst recession since WW-II: World Bank

Source: The Economic Times, 9th June 2020

- Job loss is the most severe immediate impact of Covid -19.
- India is staring at its first recession in 40 years.
- 25% Indians willing to stop insurance premiums

Source: The Economic Times, 19th June 2020

- Stocks most overvalued since 1998

Source: Economic Times, 17th June 2020

- 57 % large cap funds fail to beat their benchmarks over 20 years.

Source: Economic Times, 17th June 2020

- Tourism Sector Could Lose 174 m Jobs This Year, says WTTC report.

Source: The Economic Times, 31st Oct 2020

- Life, Medical Insurance Set to Become Dearer 20-30% hike likely due to higher risk perception, greater regulatory compliance and rising reinsurance rates

Source: The Economic Times, 24th June 2020

- PPF rate may fall below 7% to a 46 year low

Source: The Economic Times, 24th June 2020

- Mutual Fund Investors give middleman the slip

Source: The Economic Times, 30th June 2020

The Competition is getting fierce

While many among us are struggling to find out a way to survive and grow in the business in the new normal post-Covid-19 environment, new players with technological background have emerged as clear winners with the help of their startup projects.

Policybazaar (promoted by three individuals having no insurance background whatsoever) has moved from a policy price comparison website to an insurance-selling operation. The company claims to process nearly 25% of India's life insurance and over 7% of the country's retail health cover.

The Valuation of this company as on now is close to $2b (Rs. 15000 Crs.).

Source : The Economic Times, 23rd Nov 2020

This is just in the span of 12 years!

Can you believe it?

Internet Businesses Rush in as the Pandemic Widens Insurance Market.

Source: The Economic Times, 11th Sept. 2020

Amazon, which sells insurance on its platform, has applied for an insurance brokerage license, which will allow it to become an online aggregator and distributor of products. To sell a host of insurance products in the motor and liability segments, Amazon now partners with general insurance startup Acko which is backed by Infosys founder N.R. Narayana Murthy.

Flipkart, Amazon, Ola, Paytm, Phonepe, Freecharge - all the companies are selling diversified policies.

WhatsApp and Google are said to be conducting pilots to gain expertise.

Plans Ahead

- Cos. are shoring up partnerships.
- Investing in technology.

Building resources to foray into this space.

Friends, all these will certainly make our lives more challenging!!!

Chapter 10

Business Pyramid: LIC of India

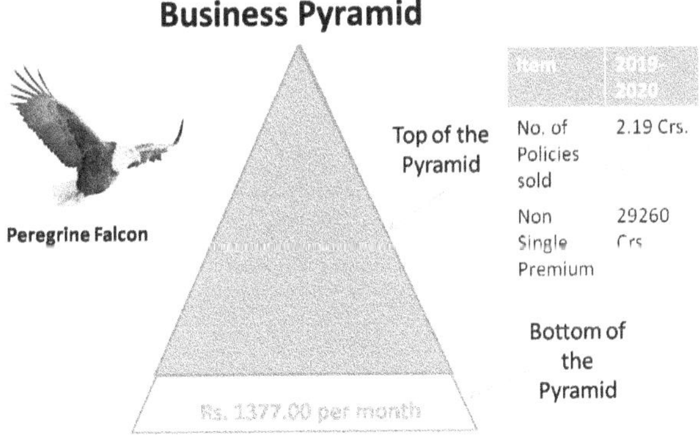

The Present Reality & The Challenges Ahead:

1. 99% Insurance Sellers work at the bottom of the pyramid with an average premium ticket size of Rs.1,377.00 per

month/Rs.16,524.00 per annum.

2. The entire space is hugely crowded.
3. People in this segment are worst affected under Covid-19 environment. They hardly have money to buy fresh insurance. In fact, they are simply struggling to survive.
4. As per the research:

   (a)The penetration of the Indian market by all insurance cos. put together is very low.

   3.69 % v/s Avg. 7% of the world.

   (b)The average Insurance per person is abysmally low (grossly under insured).
5. The saving products offered in this segment are losing their relevance because under the rapidly falling interest rate scenario the returns on such products will find it difficult to match the prevailing rate of inflation.
6. One will have to quickly learn to sell need-based protection oriented products.

Chapter 11

Opportunities Are Right in Front of You

And yet when I move into the market as a lone ranger I find HNIs are looking for us.

Where are you?

I can visualize rarest of the rare opportunities in front of us due to the following factors:

- There is an increasing degree of awareness for insurance products across the world on account of Covid-19 pandemic.
- Despite adverse circumstances, Rich is getting Richer.

  Wealth of India's Rich grows despite pandemic led headwinds.

Source: The Economic Times, 30th Sept. 2020

- Reliance could collect Rs. 1.86 Lakhs Cr. for 25.24% stake in just 58 days during a period of Covid-19. Because it converted itself from Commodity Co. to Technology Co.

LIC's disinvestment Target – 2.11 Lacs Crs.

- This clearly indicates that the market is loaded with money. It is going from one hand to another. We need to find out whether it is our hand.
- The entire segment viz. Top of the Pyramid remains wide open waiting for somebody to offer products that it needs.

Change is the need of an hour. Unless we accept the Reality and Re-align quickly with it we will soon become completely out of the place.

The irony is only a handful players have requisite knowledge/ wherewithal to unlock the huge potential untapped in this segment.

Clearly, it's the time to quickly reinvent ourselves.

Simply put, it is now survival of the QUICKEST.

Chapter 12

We Are Left With Two Options

Friends, we have 2 alternatives in front of us;

1. Get out

   OR

2. Innovate

Chapter 13

Way Forward

Before I suggest a solution let us understand the following basic Buying Principles:

1. People don't want to be sold. They want to buy.
2. Create a buying environment.
3. Your buyer should truly believe that the situation is real and there is a way to resolve it.
4. He should further believe this product can transform his life.
5. Examine carefully the Price v/s Protection offered to him.
6. Remember, buyers do not have sufficient commitment for long-term savings. Give them comfort.

7. Offer them fair value for the money they pay.
8. Do not forget there is an increasing degree of awareness in terms of Protection v/s Investments.

Chapter 14

6 Secrets of Selling 100.00 cr (1Billion) Insurance To HNIs With Ease

Here are the Six Secrets that will surely enable you to sell 100 Cr (1 Billion) Insurance to HNIs with ease

Chapter 15

Secret-1
Know Your Potential Buyers

Define the characteristics of your qualified leads & Know their Deep-Rooted Secret Desires (Needs)

Who could be my Client?

Define your potential clientele.

If you can't define them, you can't find them.

Not anybody and everybody who has money can be your potential buyer.

The surest way to succeed in selling high-value insurance to HNIs is to ensure that you are working with FIT only. Your potential buyer should truly match your value system.

Your ideal client is your own reflection.

Based on my years of experience, I have worked out six distinct characteristics of such potential buyers.

1. He/She should preferably be a Business Owner/ Promoter of a Business Enterprise having a successful track record.
2. He/She should be well qualified and preferably a 1st Generation Entrepreneur.
3. His/Her business must make profits consistently.
4. Persons with a huge appetite for bigger risks for the sake of fulfilment of their ambitions.
5. Business having Secured Liabilities/Personal Guarantees of the Business Owners.
6. Preferred Age group around 45.

Know their Deep-Rooted Secret Desires (Needs)

Remember, to influence your potential buyers you need to know their

Deep-Rooted Secret Desires (Needs)

The deep-rooted secret desires, aspirations (needs) and insecurities of HNIs are different than that of a common person.

A common person buys insurance primarily to secure the followings in case of an eventuality.

1. Replacement of Income
2. Children's Marriage
3. Children's Education

4. Adequate resources for retirement so as to live a life of dignity and financial independence

A large chunk of insurance-cum-saving products is being sold in this segment.

However, these are not the primary needs/insecurities for HNIs.

Their deep-rooted secret desires (needs) are different.

Like most Business Owners of Small & Medium scale Enterprises HNIs are:

- Worried that their Business Risks will spill over their family lives and engulf all that they have accumulated during the lifetime.
- Looking for a tightly-knit succession strategy for their businesses.
- Eager to make sure their businesses continue in their absence without having any adverse impact on their Enterprise Value.
- Desiring to Hedge Business Liabilities and Personal Guarantees.
- Intending to ensure that money is there in case their business suddenly runs out of cash and is almost on the verge of Business Insolvency.
- Planning to ensure Lifelong Financial Independence and life of Dignity.
- Designing to create a Financial Estate and a Legacy for future generation.
- Willing to make a positive mark to leave fond memories behind.

In short, they are looking for an adequate need-based Financial Business Continuity Plan that can mitigate the above-mentioned Risks/Insecurities and help them live without any worries.

Chapter 16

Secret-2 Where and How would You Find Them?

They are all around you.

Your primary sources of reaching to HNIs are as under:

1. **The Data that you own**

   E.g.:

   (a) Your Existing Customers.

   (b) Your Past Customers.

   (c) Unconverted Leads.

   (d) Database that you own or had bought previously.

(e) Their Business Cards.

(f) Your Fans and Followers on Social Media.

Remember, this is indeed your **Gold Mine** and Biggest Asset.

Do not worry whether each one of them could be your potential buyer or not because even if they don't buy they can act as an influencer and refer you further.

2. **Joint Venture**

   These are the people who have the database you are looking for.

   E.g.:

   (a) Chartered Accountants

   (b) Consultants

   (c) Lawyers/Solicitors

   (d) Socially Influencers

   (e) Heads of the Associations

   (f) CEO Groups

   (g) Trainers

Remember, the money is not simply in the 'LIST' instead it is in the relationship that you have with the list.

A well thought out cultivated relationships with Joint Ventures could be a true game changer. They will give you an Audience in abundance.

Chapter 17

Secret-3
Build a Strong Foundation

"The important thing is that you've got a strong foundation before you start to try to save the world or help other people."

–Richard Branson

You should be perceived as an Authority or an Expert in the subject else you will be treated as a commodity.

What is a Strong Foundation?

Having all or few of the followings will help you to stand out from the crowd and will give you a distinct identity as an Authority or an Expert:

1. Effective Website/Landing Page
2. Powerful Testimonials
3. Meaningful Business Card/Logo/Tag Line – Describing your USP
4. The content you are sharing
5. Innovative product presentation
6. After-sales service
7. Your commitment and value
8. Your own database
9. Personal brand page
10. A Book that you have authored
11. Your own Youtube Channel
12. A Habit of constant innovation

Chapter 18

Secret-4
You Need to be Perceived as an Expert

How can you be perceived as an Authority or an Expert and establish a truly professional relationship with your buyers?

Following sales letters have helped me and my trainees to be perceived as Champions; they have also helped in establishing relationships with our prospects.

Eventually, we all have ended up closing Big Ticket insurances.

Letter-1

Sub: Golden Rule of Asset Allocation.

Dear Sir,

Sorry to abruptly land in your inbox.

I just wanted to inform you times are difficult.

Rough seas demand abundant caution.

It is important for investors to embrace risk even if they have not experienced it and we need a lot of advisors for a lot of people who need to do hand-holding.

Diversification is crucial to investing.

It's time to examine and re-balance the avenues available for investments.

Fixed Deposits

Interest rates on Fixed Deposits in banks are falling as never before. They are unlikely to go up in a hurry. The Post Tax Returns are paltry. Not enough to out beat the retail inflation rate. This would surely destroy your wealth.

	eCircular Department: IT. ASSET LIABILITY MANAGEMENT SI.No.: 198/2020 -21 Circular No.: CFO/IT-ALM-INTEREST/4/2020-21 Date : Tue 26 May 2020

Date: 26th May, 2020

The Chief General Manager,
State Bank of India,
All Circles/CAG/CCG/SARG

Dear Sir/ Madam,

REVISION IN INTEREST RATES ON DOMESTIC RETAIL TERM DEPOSITS (BELOW RUPEES TWO CRORES) W.E.F. 27th MAY, 2020

Please refer to our Circular No. CFO/IT-ALM-INTEREST/3/2020-21 Dated 8th May, 2020 advising changes in interest rates on Domestic Retail Term Deposits.

It has now been decided to revise the interest rates for **Domestic Retail Term Deposits 'Below Rupees Two Crores'** w.e.f. **27th May, 2020** as under:

Retail Term Deposits (Below Rs. Two Crores)

(Rates in % per annum)

Tenors	**Existing Rates for Public w.e.f.**	**Revised Rates for Public w.e.f. 27/05/2020**	**Existing Rates for Senior Citizen w.e.f. 12/05/2020**	**Revised Rates for Senior Citizen w.e.f. 27/05/2020**
7 days to 45 days	**3.30**	2.90	3.80	**3.40**
46 days to 179 days	**4.30**	3.90	4.80	**4.40**
180 days to 210 days	**4.80**	4.40	5.30	**4.90**
211 days to less than 1 year	4.80	4.40	5.30	4.90
1 Year to less than 2 year	**5.50**	5.10	6.00	**5.60**

2 Years to less than 3 years	**5.50**	5.10	6.00	**5.60**
3 Years to less than 5 years	**5.70**	5.30	6.20	**5.80**
5 Years and up to 10 years	**5.70**	5.40	6.50	**6.20**

High Rated Debt Funds

What is the current YTM (Yield to Maturity) on High Rated Debt Funds?

Funds India Select Debt Funds	YTM (Aug.2020)
0 to 1-Year Bucket	**4.0%**
1 to 3-year Bucket	**5.5%**

Source: The Economic Times, 27th Oct 2020

Liquid Funds

The current rate of return on Liquid Funds ranges between 3-3.5% as compared to 5-5.5% a year ago. And, therefore, investors are putting money in other categories.

Source: The Economic Times, 10th Nov 2020

Mutual Funds

Mutual Funds have been a gateway into equity. They have not given great returns over the last few years.

Performance by Category

Category	1Yr	3Yr	5Yr	10Yr
Large cap	4.27	4.95	6.26	8.25
Midcap	11.79	1.72	5.46	11.57
Small cap	12.67	-1.29	5.02	9.45
Contra	3.70	0.21	4.88	9.24

(Figures in x*)* *Source: Value Research*

Source: The Economic Times, 3rd Sep 2020

Direct Equity

Sensex heading towards all time high despite all as mentioned below:

1. Lockdowns
2. No Stimulus
3. -23% GDP Growth
4. Highest ever NPAs
5. Highest ever unemployment
6. Uncertainty – High
7. Consumer Sentiment – Weak
8. Fear of World War-3

The Sensex trailing P/E is greater than 30 which is 46% above 10 years average.

The Sensex forward P/E is greater than 21 which is 34% above 10 years average.

Source: ET Wealth, 19th Oct 2020

Clearly, it's a time to book some profits.

The long term investment always requires a proper Asset Allocation by determining the risk level of the investor, avoiding the concentration of particular assets and getting familiar with the probability of downside risks of sudden shock.

No wonder investors have pulled out a total of Rs. 9939 Crs. from Equity Mutual Funds over the last 4 months.

Source: The Economic Times, 10th Nov 2020

Right Asset allocation is the key.

Lower Risk and Higher Safety is driving investors to look for other avenues for investments.

A million dollar question - Where do people go now as the experience in the various modes of investments has fallen short of expectations?

What should you do now?

The evergreen Golden Rule of Asset Allocation is
"When the going is good book some profits and allocate into a
Safe,
Assured,
Offering Lifetime Protection
Tax Free Returns
Supported by Sovereign Guarantee of the Govt. of India."

This is indeed our honest endeavor to help you to make informed decisions based on our credible research of the last 45 years.

We are India's Top Financial Business Continuity Planner.

Need more information?

Call us or write back to us for an **Absolutely Free Consultation.**

You have no obligation whatsoever.

We will always respect your decision even if we are not working together.

We look forward to hear from you

Warm Regards,

Letter - 2

Sub: Why Tax Free Returns are now relevant in India? Read more…

Dear Sir,

Sorry to abruptly land in your inbox.

I just wanted to inform you that it is a time to clearly understand that never before the Tax Free Returns on investments backed by the Govt. of India have assumed the importance that they truly deserve.

Look at the Current Scenario:

1. Interest rates on Bank FDs, Debt Funds are at their downward trajectories. Post Tax Returns on these instruments are not good enough to beat even the retail inflation rate.

2. The Mutual Funds have failed to register the promised Post Tax Returns and are much below the expectations considering high risk involved in such investments.
3. India falls into lowest tax regime in terms of personal income tax as compared to other developed countries as shown below:

Country	IT Rates %
Australia	45
Canada	44.5 to 54
Germany	47.47
UK	45
USA	51.8
Nepal	36
India	30

In the midst of Covid-19 chaos and major disruptions in the economic environment voices are emerging from across the world to hike personal income tax rates for HNIs.

Look at the following News

"Income Inequality

The rising income inequality has provoked sharp responses from many progressive politicians and critics on the left. U.S. Senator Bernie Sanders earlier this month introduced legislation to tax 'extreme' wealth gains during the coronavirus crisis."

Source : the Economic Times, 27th Aug 2020

"British FM Rishi Sunak 'Planning Major Tax Hikes to pay for Recovery"

Source : The Economic Times, 31st Aug 2020

There are enough reasons to believe that India will follow the suit sooner rather than later.

Under these circumstances it is difficult to ignore any opportunity of investment Guaranteed by Govt. of India offering decent Tax Free Returns.

The wisdom demands that it is a time to reshuffle your Asset Allocation and invest at least a portion out of your current financial investments in such instruments.

Call us or write back to us for an **Absolutely Free Consultation.**

We are India's Top Financial Business Continuity Planner.

We look forward to hear from you

Warm Regards,

These truly meaningful educational messages used at regular intervals have brought me closer to my clients. They all perceive me as an Authority in the subject and are now eager to take my advice.

You can watch my LIVE Sales Call on Youtube by using following link:

https://www.youtube.com/watch?v=JbYEufVoNnM

Chapter 19

Secret-5 Build Professional Relationship, Trust or Faith with Your Potential Buyers

Remember, trust and credibility are the only currency we are dealing in.

How do we create trust/faith/relationship?

Your strong foundation will certainly help you to create a first step to build up trust/faith/relationship.

One of the effective ways of building up relationships is to author a book, call them in a webinar or send them educational messages touching upon their deep-rooted secret desires (Needs).

Remember, your every act or written communication should be meaningful. Your buyer should be able to relate with it.

This will create affinity and liking for you. The more you communicate in a meaningful manner, the more you start building affinity and relationship.

Building up trust/faith/relationship takes time. Therefore, your every act or conversation must bring micro-transformation in the minds of buyers.

Your potential buyers should relate with challenges you may mention in your communication.

Chapter 20

Secret-6 (a) Make An Irresistible Sales Offer

What is an Irresistible Offer (IRO)?

It's all about value creation. Your client should truly believe that it is the best available offer and that **There is No Other Alternative (TINA Factor).**

Your offer should be too attractive or tempting to deny. It should create an impulse of buying.

99% people do not give Irresistible Offer and, therefore, you can stand out in the crowd. It gives you free mouth publicity and amplifies your growth, only if you apply it.

Your Irresistible Offer can be from your product line or it can be from your non-product line.

Your offer should create a scarcity and a **Fear Of Missing Out (FOMO Factor)** in the minds of buyers making them feel if they do not buy **NOW** they will incur a big loss.

Chapter 21

Secret-6 (b) Learn the Art of Conversational Selling (बातचीत)

Think of a time when you convinced your friend for something you truly believed that could add value in his life, e.g., to watch a movie or to undergo a training course.

Now watch that process in slow motion from start to finish. Watch all you did. Visualize everything you did till you received a 'YES'.

Notice those major milestones.

E.g.

(a) First you create an environment

(b) Order a cup of coffee

(c) Begin with a light talk

(d) Come to the main point

(e) Objection Handling

(f) Second Meet

(g) Third Meet

Write down all the steps that you took to convince him.

Now think one of your times when you convinced your clients.

See the difference, if any.

Friends, let me assure you the Secrets that I have shared with you in this book are sure shot practical solutions that can bring results if applied the way it should be.

Chapter 22

And Now Back To The Case Study…

I know, you might be wondering how can I leave you midway, without speaking about something that I really wanted you to know. So here it is.

By now, I am sure, you must be eager to know as to what solutions I proposed that made my prospect accept my offer without raising further objections.

Here is a complete framework of the solution.

- I did my homework to understand my prospect's deep-rooted secret desires (needs) and insecurities.
- I studied the Annual Reports and the future projections of the company.
- Based on the above, I worked out a **Protection Valuation** of the company.

My Findings

- The company had laid out a well thought out Business Continuity Plan and Hedged a few of the Financial Risks.
- What was still missing was a provision of full-proof **Succession Plan.**

What a full-proof Succession Plan would mean to any Business?

Simply put, a full-proof Succession Plan designed by us will offer two solutions in the eventuality of a permanent departure of key driving force in the business on account of death:

Solution–1

The successor wants to run the business.

We will make sure that if the successor of the key driving force decides to run the business, he or she should be able to run it even better than the key person before them.

Solution–2

The successor wants to sell the business.

We will ensure a decent exit route making sure that the successor gets all the dues accruing to his business without having any adverse impact on the **Enterprise Valuation.**

What is Protection Valuation of the Business?

The **Protection Valuation** of the Business is different than that of the **Enterprise Valuation**.

A **Protection Valuation** of the Business is defined as under: It is an amount that the Business would need

- To ensure smooth continuity of the business and

- Will protect the Enterprise Value of the business even in the eventuality of permanent departure of key functionaries in the business.

What is an Enterprise Value of the Business?

It is the perceived value of the Business Enterprise that a buyer would like to pay based on the Current and the Future earning potentials.

Here is how my 1-to-1 conversation with the prospect took place

Me: Sir, you have a great going. Do you know the Enterprise Value of your business?

Prospect: (Pat come the reply) Yes. I do know. It is Rs. 250.00 cr, at least.

Me: How did you arrive at this figure?

Prospect: Based on the current and future earning potential of the business.

Me: What is your role in building up this business and bringing it to the scale where it stands now?

Prospect: Yes. I know. I have played a major role to build it up at the scale where it is now.

Me: Let me confirm and put it in other words what you have said now.

"The present pleasant state of your business is the sheer outcome of your Vision, Risk Taking Ability and the Quality of Leadership. But, for you, perhaps the company would not have reached where it is now."

These are the rarest of the rare virtues that any successful entrepreneur possesses and that you are definitely one of them.

Prospect: God is kind to me.

Me: You will agree that nobody knows your Business better than you.

Prospect: Yes.

Me: Can anyone of your employees replace you instantly and effectively in case of an eventuality?

Prospect: Perhaps No.

Me: Will it not have an adverse impact on the working of the company?

Prospect: Probably Yes.

Me: Do you agree that the Enterprise Value of your business is not a sum total of brick and mortar that your company possesses?

It is the perception in terms of future earnings of your business that decides the Enterprise Value of your company.

Prospect: Yes. I tend to agree.

Me: Do you agree in that case there would be major erosion in the Enterprise Value of your business and, therefore, you must work out a solution to ensure that your business continues to remain most valuable in financial terms so as to fulfill the following two objectives:

(a) Your company will continue to attract and retain the top talents in the industry.

(b) Provide a decent exit route to your successors should they want to get out of the business by ensuring protection of the Enterprise Value of the business.

Prospect: "Yes. I do agree with you.

However, what is the cost involved in initiating such a protective device vis-à-vis the value that it would offer?"

Me: This is indeed a legitimate question.

Let me inform you-

How does the cost involved compare with the value that it offers?

The answer is simple.

All you need to do is save a miniscule portion from your Business Cash Flow.

Remember, a small amount saved year-on-year will deliver money when it is needed MOST, when no one else will respond or help.

In other words, our Financial Business Continuity Plan would protect your

Business, Family and Old Age.

Prospect: That sounds good. We can go ahead.

Friends, this was an emphatic Yes. He found my offer truly logical and Irresistible.

Rest was just a formality.

A cheque of Rs.121 Lakhs was handed over and the deal was successfully sealed.

Chapter 23

A Thanks Letter Worth Million Dollar

To Create a Permanent Place in the Hearts of the Buyers

This is how I cement permanent professional relationships with my clients.

Sub: We are the Trustee of your Wealth.

Dear Sir,

Please accept our appreciation and sincere Thanks for letting us serve you.

By virtue of our advice you have in fact, in a way, created a **TRUST** for the members of your family whose Financial Worth is more than Rs.150.00 cr!!!

And, you have made us the **TRUSTEE** of this invaluable Asset.

The security and wellbeing of your family is now Our Responsibility.

Sometimes in the rush of business life we fail to say **THANKS** loud enough.

But you can be sure your patronage is never taken for granted. Our aim is to please and satisfy you.

To serve you is a Real Privilege.

Regards,

Randhir Bhalla

And here is an illustrative reply from my Client:

Dear Mr. Randhir Bhalla,

Pleasure and Thanks a lot for your valued effort Sir.

We appreciate the same and wish you all the best for future.

We sincerely look forward to grow together.

Truly Yours,

Chapter 24

Recap

Phew!

Finally, we have come to an end so let's recap what we learnt till now.

1. Times are testing. However, there is enough money in the market. It is up to us to turn the present crisis into a great opportunity.
2. The current pandemic has sharply enhanced perception of importance of Risk Mitigation Devices. You need to look at this with an eye of optimism.
3. You need to change marketing strategies to create a buying environment.
4. As advisors our currency is trust. Never manipulate. Only influence.

5. You should be perceived as an expert so that you can stand out otherwise people will treat you as a commodity.
6. You should never stop learning. Learn from Real Experts or Actual Practitioners who have experienced the real world of hardcore Big Selling.

Chapter 25

Friends You Have Two Choices

There are two choices right in front of you:

1. Conquer every roadblock and Do it Yourself.

OR

2. Have me by your side and make sure you are doing it right.

Learn from the Maestros

From Whom Would You Like To Learn Cricket?

A Club Cricketer OR Sunil Gavaskar

Chapter 26

This is What a Few of My Trainees Have Said

I sincerely thank my Trainees who have whole-heartedly acknowledged the efforts I put in my Training Programs to make them Champions in true sense.

Ravindra Kumar

Regional Manager, LIC of India

"Friends,

It is Truly Magical

I want to share something with all of you.

During the last 2 months, I have been attending regularly the training sessions of Mr. Randhir Bhalla.

The knowledge imparted in this program is truly of an international class.

In my entire career I have never come across any trainer who distributes deep rooted knowledge without any reservations with a single minded mission to uplift the entire insurance community.

I am indeed privileged to witness the change that is happening in front of me."

***

Ramesh Damani

Country's Leading Life and General Insurance Advisor Kolkata

"This is just Superb !!!

Learning at any stage of your

life is inevitable.

This in fact is the secret of my success.

Just do it and learn from this class."

***

Bhushan Suhas Limye

Mumbai, Holding 15th Rank in all India

"The Educational Email Marketing taught by Mr. Randhir Bhalla and the entire process chart suggested by him are unbelievable.

It is simply a Wow experience!!!

There is a magical change in my business. The new businesses are just pouring in.

My Total FP for the month of Sep 2020 is more than Rs. 8.00 Crs."

***

Bhaurao Yeshwant Pingle

(Nashik)

"Within 3 days I got 18 Lakh FP in Traditional plan...

He is trying to change old Belief system ....

WIN : What is New ???

New (थिंकिंग) pattern...

New Powerful Self Talk...

Upto Month End my COT will be declared...

Thank you to Bhalla Sir"

***

Mr. Himanshu Shah

I have retired as SR.DM from Vadodara.

I watched your entire program.

No words other than Excellent. I wish you grand success in this endeavor.

Thanks

***

G P Sharma

(Chandigarh)

"Your training is my lifeline.

Otherwise I had lost hope of Big Business.

Thank you very much Sir.

I am so much Excited."

***

Kirankumar Amballa

(Mumbai)

I have attended almost all Trainers Workshops in the last 21 years of my Agency since 1999.

You are the only one in INDIA who is Teaching us to win the Battles within ourselves and outside....

You are among the Handful people in our Country who have Decoded the Art of Selling to the Ultra HNIs....

But you are the only one who is sharing this Trade Secret with your Fraternity.

We can't thank you enough Randhir Bhalla sir. Just hope that our association with you continues beyond this course

Best Wishes.... Much Respect.... Tons of Gratitude.... Lots of Love,

***

Chapter 27

Our Ultimate Sales Skills (USS) Training Programs

If you are willing to come into my world join our Ultimate Sales Skills (USS) Training Programs.

What you will learn in this program?

This program essentially focuses on Innovation.

It is designed to bring about desired changes by sharing with you unique tools and techniques that are taught in the top business schools of the world.

I am going to share all these things that I have learnt during my last 45 years of corporate experience.

This program is designed to take you to the next level by:

1. Showing you where the money lies.
2. How to trace people with money.
3. How to build everlasting relationship with buyers.
4. How to create an environment whereby your prospects will prefer to buy YOUR CONCEPT and also ONLY FROM YOU.
5. How to prepare an Offer that is Irresistible
6. And finally, how to seek ~~references~~/recommendations from them.

Friends, I want to assure you that the entire curriculum is designed to add huge value in your personal and professional lives and will help you to surpass all your previous goals and aspirations you have simply dreamt about.

It's all about choices you make in life.

Make the right one.

"Sometimes it's the smallest decisions that can change your life forever."

–Keri Russell

To know further about our proposed Training Programs please contact us:

Email id: randhirbhalla1950@gmail.com

Mb.: 9376117563, 8141117563

CALL TO ACTION

I want to provide training sessions to you and educate on how to sell Rs.100.00 cr (1 Billion) and more. I am sure, these training sessions will prove to be a thing of beauty, that will keep on giving you joy in the coming months, coming years, always. Given below is the format of bonus, exclusively given to my readers:

Bonus for 1000 early subscribers:

1. 2 Free Training Sessions of 2:30 Hrs each by Mr. Randhir Bhalla–Worth **Rs. 43000**

And

2. 2 Free Joint Calls–Worth **Rs. Invaluable**

This is a limited time offer; as the day the seat will get filled, I will have no option left than to close the offer.

Please book NOW.

And register your Name, City, and Mail Address by sending a WhatsApp Message on following Nos. and links:

8141117563, 9376117563

randhirbhalla1950@gmail.com

http://www.randhirbhallaandassociates.com/

https://www.youtube.com/watch?v=JbYEufVoNnM

www.ingramcontent.com/pod-product-compliance
Ingram Content Group UK Ltd.
Pitfield, Milton Keynes, MK11 3LW, UK
UKHW021656190726
13853UKWH00001B/289